Love your bump

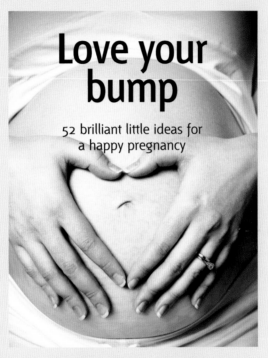

Love your bump

52 brilliant little ideas for a happy pregnancy

Lynn Huggins-Cooper

brilliantideas

CAREFUL NOW

It should go without saying that the advice in this book should not be thought of as a substitute for the professional help you can get from your doctor and midwife. Please see these ideas as food for thought and not suggestions for a plan of action. If you're thinking of taking any supplements, trying out some exercises or using any remedies check it out with the professionals first. Neither the author nor the publisher can be held responsible for circumstances arising from use or misuse of the information in this book. All web addresses were correct at time of going to press but in this fast moving world some may have changed – we're really sorry for any inconvenience this may cause.

First published in 2007 by
The Infinite Ideas Company Limited
36 St Giles
Oxford, OX1 3LD
United Kingdom
www.infideas.com

A CIP catalogue record for this book is available from the British Library
ISBN 978-1-905940-28-8

Designed and typeset by Baseline Arts Ltd, Oxford
Printed in China

Brilliant ideas

Introduction

From the moment that stick turns blue, you
are bombarded with so much information and
'dos and don'ts' about your pregnancy that you
can easily feel overwhelmed and confused.
Minor worries can become major fears. You become ultra sensitised
to every pregnancy scare story until it seems that nothing is safe.
Niggling worries and the stress they cause is a more common
'pregnancy complaint' than morning sickness. Your healthcare
providers are a source of much information and guidance, but that
can be focused mainly on the physical side of pregnancy, leaving
many questions unanswered and your concerns seeming trivial. You
may also find that you are whisked through your appointments so
quickly that you forget what you wanted to ask.

That's where this book helps. It's not written by a midwife or an
obstetrician. It's written by a parent, just like you. A mother who has
been pregnant four times and has felt the same sense of confusion
and questions as you.

The tips and advice in this book come from years of experience – mine, and that of friends, family and of the many women I meet in the course of my work. Being pregnant connects us to all the other women who are – and have been – pregnant. Pregnancy is a great leveller, as you learn to blithely discuss your nipples, flatulence and haemorrhoids with near strangers!

This book aims to empower you at a time when it is all too easy to feel like a 'baby receptacle'. So don't spoil this blissfully happy experience with 'what ifs' and worries – put your feet up (you may as well make the most of being pregnant) with this book and prepare to enjoy it!

1. You're pregnant!

What changes can you expect immediately?

Queasiness, frequent peeing and tiredness can take the shine off early pregnancy. But rest assured – there are ways of making life easier.

As soon as you get pregnant, your body goes into overdrive – so no wonder you're tired and possibly weepy. Your body has to cope with creating the placenta – the powerhouse of pregnancy, and your baby's life-support system – so your lethargy is quite legitimate. It only lasts while your body adjusts and the placenta is formed. By the second trimester, you will have more energy. Try to manage your day to build in as much rest as possible and keep domestic chores to a minimum.

Frequent peeing can be a real nuisance in early pregnancy. It is due to the increase in body fluids that occur at this time. As your pregnancy advances, you may find that the pressure of the uterus

Here's an idea for you

Sea-bands are elastic straps with plastic studs that are worn on each wrist to depress the acupressure point that relieves nausea. They are non-invasive and have no effect on your baby. You can buy them at any large chemists.

makes you want to pee more. Don't be tempted to drink less – drink six–eight glasses of water a day. Your pee should be light or colourless: if it looks dark, you are not drinking enough.

Morning sickness can be the worst part of early pregnancy. For an unlucky few, the nausea and sickness can last longer. Hyperemesis gravidarum is a serious condition affecting 1 in 200 pregnancies. Excessive vomiting, more common with twins and in first pregnancies, can be debilitating and even end in temporary hospitalisation. If you are vomiting excessively, consult your healthcare provider.

'Morning sickness' is a misnomer as it can strike at any time. Possibly the reason why many women suffer in the morning is the fact that their stomach is empty. Try to:

- Eat something every few hours.
- Keep a tin of crackers by the bed to eat first thing.
- Drink camomile, ginger or peppermint tea.
- Avoid cooking smells if this causes nausea.
- Eat bland foods.

2. The risks

Putting perils into perspective.

How much alcohol is safe during pregnancy?
None really. When you drink alcohol, it enters the foetal
bloodstream in the same concentration as it enters yours. It takes
your baby twice as long to eliminate it. Foetal alcohol syndrome
(FAS) – where the babies of heavy drinkers are born with problems
such as malformation of the head, limbs, heart and nervous system
– has been called 'the hangover that lasts a lifetime'. It only takes
five–six units a day for FAS to develop. More moderate drinkers
increase the risk of foetal alcohol effect, where behavioural and
developmental problems can occur. You also increase the risk of
miscarriage and low birth weight.

The babies of smokers are more
likely to be lower birth weight,
and to suffer from asthma and
chest infections – and are more
likely to be victims of sudden
infant death syndrome (cot death).
Smoke poisons your baby with

Here's an idea for you

If you do feel tempted to smoke, dig
out the cute little baby clothes you
haven't been able to resist in a bid to
put you off. You won't want the baby
clothes to reek as though junior spent
the night clubbing.

carbon monoxide, and reduces the oxygen that he or she receives through the placenta. Smoking in pregnancy may even reduce the likelihood of you becoming grandparents. A Danish study found that baby boys exposed to smoke in utero grow into men with a 25% below average sperm count.

Toxoplasmosis is a serious infection that can cause miscarriage and abnormalities. It may be found in cat poop so take precautions. This is not a good time to get a new cat. If you already have one, make sure you wear disposable gloves to change the litter tray or avoid doing it. It is likely that you have been exposed to toxoplasmosis at some time and have immunity, but take no risks. Wear gloves when you garden. Make sure any home-grown produce are well washed.

3. Build a better baby

Nutrition during pregnancy.

Ensure you are eating a broad range of food encompassing all the food groups. This way you make sure that your baby gets everything they need for optimum development.

A pregnant woman needs 75–80 g of protein a day. Hard cheeses, lean meat, cooked fish, pulses, soya beans and eggs are all good sources. Protein is the building block for human cells – and that includes your baby, as well as you! Avoid blue-veined cheese, mould-ripened soft cheese such as brie and soft, unpasturised goat and sheep cheese due to the risk of listeria, a type of food poisoning.

Calcium is vital for the development of muscles and nerves, blood clotting and enzyme activity. It is needed for building strong bones and teeth. Adult women need around 1,000 mg of calcium a day, and pregnant women need a little more. One glass of milk provides about 300 mg of calcium. Other good sources are cottage cheese, yoghurt, sardines and salmon, kale and tofu.

Here's an idea for you

Keep a 'food log'. It will help you to have an overview to make sure you are eating enough of the right foods.

Complex carbohydrates will give you a great source of slow burn energy. They also help to prevent constipation. Choose whole-wheat bread, cereal, pasta and rice. Beans and peas, fresh fruit and vegetables are also good sources.

Other important nutrients you need in pregnancy include vitamin D, iron, vitamin B12, zinc and folic acid. Your vitamin B12 needs are higher in pregnancy due to vitamin B12's role in tissue creation and the building of DNA – and you're making a whole new person! The recommended daily allowance (RDA) in pregnancy is 2.2 micrograms. One source of vitamin B12 is fortified cereal. Alternatively try meat, dairy products and eggs, and fermented soya products such as miso and tamari.

Good sources of vitamin C include fruits and vegetables such as oranges, strawberries, tomatoes, peppers and cabbage.

Include iron-rich foods in your diet. Your baby needs iron for the development of its blood supply. Foods high in iron include cashew nuts, carob, beef, pulses and wholewheat cereals. Drinking orange juice will help you to absorb the iron in your food more readily. Make sure you consume enough essential fatty acids (EFAs) – found in oily fish – to help the development of your baby's brain. Walnuts, wholegrains, green leafy vegetables and rapeseed oil are also good sources.

4. Moody momma

Coping with anxiety and mood swings.

After the first elation – or shock – of finding
out that you are pregnant, you may find yourself feeling flat. It's hard
to feel positive when you are feeling tired and sick. You may find that
you are uncharacteristically moody and irrational. This is partially due
to the massive surge of hormones experienced at the beginning of
pregnancy – but may also be due to the mental adjustment needed to
see yourself as a mother.

Antenatal clinics are a great source of support, not just from medical
staff, but from other women. Talk to
your partner about your worries. If
you are concerned about how you
will cope with a baby and your
career, discuss how you will deal
with childcare. If you have friends
with young children, ask how they
cope.

Here's an idea for you

Remind your partner how special she is.
She may be being the Partner From
Hell, but she really can't help it at
times. Pregnancy mood swings can be
like PMT writ large. Be reassured, she
will return to normal after the postnatal
period. Different, but normal...

For dads

Dads-to-be can feel out of their depth too. Broadly speaking, men aren't used to sharing their worries, and this can cause extra angst. Who do you talk to? Ordinarily, your first port of call would be your partner, but you may not want to burden her now. Ideally, talk to a dad you trust. It could be your own dad or a friend or relative with young children. You will probably discover that they had similar worries. Their experience of coping will help you to realise that you can cope too.

Worried about the cost of everything? Babies can't tell Prada from Primark so shop around for the best deals. Second-hand baby equipment is obviously cheaper – and babies use the frilly little baskets, etc., for such a short time that second hand looks new anyway.

5. Bump and grind

The sex question.

We don't just have sex to make babies and
that doesn't change just because we are pregnant.

Many men feel disconcerted about sex in pregnancy – there's
someone else there… Rest assured, boys; however impressively
endowed you are, your baby is cushioned within a sac of amniotic
fluid, and a plug of jelly seals the cervix to keep your baby safe.

Deep penetration is not a great idea though as your cervix may feel
ultra sensitive due to the additional blood vessels you've developed
to accommodate the increase in blood flow to the uterus.

Be prepared, boys – although
pregnancy sickness and other
discomforts of early pregnancy can
put paid to sex for a while, you may
suddenly find your partner
becomes rampant! Hormonal
changes during pregnancy can lead

Here's an idea for you

As your bump expands, remember that
sex is not all about penetration and try
some alternative forms of love making.

Defining idea

'It's one of the sexiest times in a woman's life.'
DAVID BECKHAM, talking about his then pregnant wife, Victoria

to a variety of physical changes that make sex great. Increased blood supply to your pelvic area can lead to vulval engorgement and the same type of gentle swelling that occurs as our bodies prepare for penetration. The other good news is that pregnant women have an increase in vaginal discharge. Sounds messy – but it can lead to an increased libido.

Pregnancy brings mental changes too. No worries about contraception, for a start. If you've been trying for a baby for some time, pregnancy also releases you from the anxiety of those timed, temperature-charted efforts that suck the pleasure out of sex.

Some men may feel really turned on by their partner's developing body. Others are turned off – you may be afraid of hurting your partner or the baby, or you may find it hard to reconcile your view of motherhood with your sexual partner. Making love will reassure you both that you are still sexy people – not just mummy and daddy!

6. Work it, baby!

Exercise in pregnancy – what is safe?

Gentle exercise can ease backaches, reduce the likelihood of constipation and releases the natural 'happy chemicals', endorphins, that can increase your sense of wellbeing. Many studies suggest that exercise during pregnancy helps shorten labour and birth.

If you have been very active before and are doing an activity that is safe for pregnancy, generally you can continue. However, most women are not able to maintain their same pre-pregnancy pace. If you were previously sedentary, exercise you can begin while pregnant includes walking, swimming and specialised pregnancy exercise classes.

Here's an idea for you

Your usual sports bra will fit for the first trimester, but your breasts will get larger as your pregnancy progresses. Get remeasured then. If you have big breasts to start with, try wearing a soft maternity bra under a sports bra for added support.

Always talk to your doctor before beginning any exercise programme. If you have an existing medical condition, a history of premature labour or are having a multiple birth, only the gentlest of exercise is suitable.

Begin any new regime slowly. If you feel overtired, your heart is pounding or you experience pain, stop. Make sure you don't overheat – temperatures greater than 39°C (102.6°F) can potentially cause problems with your developing baby, especially in the first three months. If the weather is hot, exercise in an air-conditioned place or wait until late afternoon or early evening.

Body changes that may affect exercising during pregnancy:

- Your respiratory rate is increased which can make you breathless.
- As your womb grows, your lower back becomes more curved. This, along with the increased weight of your boobs, causes your centre of gravity to shift. It also makes you more likely to fall.
- Your body releases a hormone called relaxin which loosens the joints of your pelvis to make it widen. This makes other joints relax and increases the risk of sprains and muscle pulls. Warm up and cool down thoroughly.
- Your blood volume increases by 40% to carry nutrients and oxygen to your baby. This increase can cause light-headedness. If you often feel giddy or breathless, consult your healthcare provider. You may be anaemic.

7. Babe or bloater?

What the best-dressed bumps are wearing.

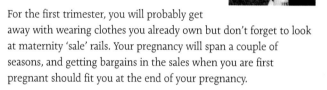

For the first trimester, you will probably get away with wearing clothes you already own but don't forget to look at maternity 'sale' rails. Your pregnancy will span a couple of seasons, and getting bargains in the sales when you are first pregnant should fit you at the end of your pregnancy.

You can also buy similar clothes to the ones you already wear in larger sizes – but be warned, it's not only your belly that grows. Your boobs can also give you a good run for your money.

To cut down on unnecessary spending purloin clothes from your partner's wardrobe like shirts and t-shirts! You may also know folks who have just had babies who will be only too pleased to lend you their gear until they need it again. Maternity wear, be warned, does not necessarily come cheap. Surf the net to check out what's available and compare prices. Look on sites such as eBay too.

Here's an idea for you

Choose natural fabrics such as cotton as you will sweat more than usual. For the same reason, dress in layers.

It is also worth buying clothes that will see you through pregnancy and nursing, if you intend to breastfeed. You can buy special tops with flaps, holes and cantilevers to pop your boob out surreptitiously as your baby needs feeding but t-shirts and jumpers lifted up to tuck the baby underneath work just fine.

You will need to buy three ultra supportive maternity bras. Don't wear a bra with an underwire – the pressure they exert has been linked to a painful condition known as non-infective mastitis, which can hinder the development of milk ducts. You will also need breastfeeding bras if you intend to feed your baby yourself. In the UK, the National Childbirth Trust has great bras and have a network of agents who will measure and fit you.

You can also buy special pregnancy knickers. Wearing cotton bikini pants in a bigger size than usual will equally do the trick.

8. Beach babe or beached whale?

Avoid 'eating for two'.

Don't look upon pregnancy as a no-holds-barred 'I'm eating for two' food fest. For the first trimester (up to 12 weeks) your body only needs about 100 extra calories a day – and that amounts to roughly a piece of fruit. During the second and third trimesters, you need about 300 extra calories per day.

Expect to gain around 11–16 kg (25–35 lb), but do not become fixated on your weight. Women who gain less than 9 kg (20 lb) tend to have smaller babies, who may even be more likely to be born prematurely. Women who gain excessive amounts equally risk their health. The muscles have to work harder the heavier you get, and this may result in back and leg pain, increased tiredness, piles, varicose veins – and even complications during delivery. Of the average of 11 kg (25 lb) of weight gained, roughly 2.5–3.5 kg

Here's an idea for you

Do not go on a crash diet. This can be positively dangerous in the postpartum period when you need optimum nutrition to cope with the stresses of new parenthood.

(6–8 lb) is the baby. Your enlarged womb weighs around a kilo and the placenta and amniotic fluid weigh about 500 g each. Another 2–4 kg of fluid are present as extra blood and fluid, and you carry an extra 2 kg of fat. Around 1.5–2 kg (3–4 lb) should be gained in the first trimester, then 5.5–6.5 kg (12–14 lb) in the second. In the last trimester, you should expect to gain around half a kilo a week. This slows off in the last few weeks, and you may find that your weight drops slightly just before delivery.

We worry about our pregnant and postnatal figures because we see celebrities in crop tops parading their neat bumps, then immediately returning to their svelte selves weeks after the birth. Remember: real women can't do this. We don't have personal trainers, chefs and nannies.

9. Love the skin you're in

Coping with your 'hormonal skin'

You may find that your skin breaks out more in pregnancy, despite all that clean living as oil (sebum) production increases. You might get spots, particularly in the last trimester. The tiny oil glands ('Montgomery's tubercles') around your nipples may also enlarge to help protect your nipples and stop them from drying out during breastfeeding. Things will return to normal after delivery.

Drink lots of water, and eat plenty of vitamin B6-rich foods to help control hormonally induced skin problems. Avoid supplements unless you have consulted your doctor. Do not take any anti-acne prescription drugs during pregnancy: they carry a high risk of causing birth defects.

Here's an idea for you

Avoid harsh exfoliants, which can aggravate your skin. Make yourself a gentle facial scrub from fine oatmeal mixed with honey and a little water. 'Press' it onto your skin before washing it off with tepid water.

Increased sweating during pregnancy may result in a sweat rash under your boobs and in your groin. Bathe the area in cool water. You can also sprinkle on cornflour to reduce chafing. As your skin stretches, you may feel generalised itching. Take warm showers and baths rather than hot. If your skin is ultra itchy, dissolve a cup of bicarbonate of soda in the bath water. If the itching is unbearable or you have a persistent rash, contact your healthcare provider.

Stretch marks are small tears made in response to the pulling and stretching your dermis undergoes as you expand. The jury is still out as to whether any of the lotions available effectively reduce them. If you do get stretch marks, try not to worry. They start off red, but fade.

You may also notice a dark line running from your pubes up to your belly button. The line is called the linea nigra, found more often in women with darker skin and hair. Pre-pregnancy, you had an unnoticeable line in the same place. When you are pregnant, you produce more melanin and that causes the line to darken. It usually disappears again after the birth.

10. Home or away?

How do you know what to choose?

Read about where people give birth, go to
hospital and birthing centre open days, and above all, talk to other
families about their experiences.

If you decide on a home birth, midwives bring everything that is
needed to your home. Statistics show that home births are as safe,
or safer, than hospital birth for women with low-risk pregnancies,
but the downside is that all the empowerment and decision making
now falls on your head. It also means you are committed to
managing your own pain – although gas and air and injected
painkillers are available, an epidural
is not.

A midwife-led birthing centre
provides an alternative if you are
not quite comfortable with home
birth, but do not want to give birth
in a hospital. If you experience
complications during labour, it's
likely that you'll need to be transferred to hospital anyway.

Here's an idea for you

When you go to hospital appointments,
write down your questions so you
remember what to ask. Make a flexible
birth plan and share it with your carers,
and give a copy to them to be attached
to your notes.

You may decide that you feel safest giving birth in hospital. For example, you have immediate access to emergency care should there be complications. The downside to hospital care is that however well furnished with cushions and duvets, they can seem clinical and even intimidating. You also have less privacy in hospital.

Although you are generally past caring, it may seem as though a never-ending stream of different faces pop in to have a peek at the 'business end'. You can feel less in control during a hospital birth, as your birth is 'medicalised', and you are more likely to have interventions in hospital such as a drip to accelerate labour, or foetal monitoring. That said, a vocal and well-informed set of parents can still ensure that they have an individual experience. Be prepared to be awkward if necessary: it's your birth and your baby.

11. Meet the midwife

Your chance to get answers to all your questions.

Your first antenatal visit, known as a 'booking-in appointment' usually takes place between about eight and twelve weeks of pregnancy and is the longest clinic visit you will experience.

The midwife will ask you a lot of questions to help her assess if your pregnancy is low risk, or if there are any potential problems. She will ask about your general health and your medical history, and the details of any health problems in both your and your partner's family, such as heart disease.

She will also ask about your obstetric history – any previous pregnancies and pregnancy losses, including those that have been terminated. You will have the opportunity to discuss where you would prefer to have your baby.

Here's an idea for you

You don't have to wait for your next appointment to speak to a midwife if something is worrying you. You will be given a 24-hour contact number at your booking visit for urgent concerns.

33

Your midwife will also ask about your ethnic origin to assess if you are at any risk of conditions such as sickle cell anaemia.

She will also ask you some questions about your lifestyle. She is not passing judgement, but is highlighting any risks to your baby. This includes whether you smoke or drink, are taking any medication; non-prescription or recreational drugs, and what work you do in case there are any hazards attached.

Your midwife will also want to know the date of your last menstrual period and the length of your monthly cycle. This will enable her to calculate your delivery date. She will also ask which contraception you used before you became pregnant.

A blood sample is taken to test your immunity to rubella, to find out your blood group, your rhesus status and whether you are anaemic. Your blood will also be tested for HIV, syphilis and hepatitis B unless you specifically ask not to have these tests.

Your urine will be tested, so take a specimen in a clean jar. Your midwife will test for protein in your urine – an early sign of pre-eclampsia. She will also check for infection and possibly sugar, which can indicate gestational diabetes.

Your blood pressure will be checked on this and every visit, and your midwife may use a Sonicaid to listen to your baby's heart.

12. The best-laid plans...

Your birth plans.

A birth plan is a list of preferences for your birth experience, to help guide your healthcare providers when you might be 'otherwise engaged'!

Start your plan by writing a list of everything you want at the birth. Rank your list, and take the top seven or eight to write into a birth plan. Your plan needs to be brief. In an ideal world, there would be plenty of time for midwives to read and digest the minutiae of your every whim – but in reality they are busy people. Think of a birth plan as a tool for opening channels of communication with your doctor or midwife.

Find out about the typical experiences of parents who have had their babies in your chosen setting. This can then be adapted to fit your

Here's an idea for you

A positive attitude will really help when you approach labour. Imagine yourself in strong labour, visualising yourself coping with the contractions in a variety of ways – breathing, changing position, being massaged – even having medication. This imagery will help you to work through any fears you have.

Defining idea

'A satisfying birth experience is directly
related to the control you feel over the
birth experience itself. Part of achieving
a sense of control comes from careful
preparation.'
CONNIE BANACK, MotherCare

wishes. Finding out about routine
care saves you cluttering up your
plan with things that will happen
anyway. Keep your plan clear and
simple, on one page. Discuss your
plan with your partner, your doula if
you are having one, and your
midwife. The birth plan should act as
a reminder of discussions had during
your pregnancy. Nothing within it
should come as a surprise.

A birth plan is not some sort of contract or guarantee of the type of birth
you will have – and neither you nor your healthcare provider is 'bound'
by it in any way. Even if things do not go according to plan, unless there
is an emergency and things have to move very fast indeed you should
still expect to be consulted about your wishes.

13. Work, rest and play

Maximising your energy levels.

First Trimester

In early pregnancy, hormonal changes can make you feel drained. Annoyingly, when this tiredness is at its worst, you don't even look pregnant! Your metabolism has increased as your body works hard to produce your baby – and that requires a lot of energy. You are also creating the placenta. Listen to your body. When it all gets too much have a nap. At work, try to cat-nap at lunchtime. If you are at home with toddlers, nap when they do. To help to boost your energy levels, eat small, frequent energy-boosting meals. If you are constantly exhausted, talk to your doctor. You may be anaemic. An iron-rich diet or herbal tonic, recommended by your healthcare provider, can help.

Here's an idea for you

Make sure you relax between contractions to conserve your energy. Sip water and suck sweets to give you an energy boost. A warm bath can also be helpful. Once you get to the stage of needing to push try different positions. Squatting or pushing on all fours can be very effective.

Defining idea

'You cannot understand what it is to be tired, until you're a parent.'
NICCI GERRARD, novelist

Second Trimester

You should feel less tired now. Many women feel really energised. But don't overdo it, and get some early nights to make up for the inevitable sleep deficit!

Third Trimester

You are putting on more weight, and this takes its toll. You may be having trouble sleeping, as it gets hard to get comfortable. Use extra pillows – the V-shaped, orthopaedic ones are good and are helpful when breastfeeding too. Ensure you are eating plenty of energising foods. Try to take naps and have a few early nights. Make sure you stay hydrated too. Drinking less won't make you pee less, but it will make you dehydrated and groggy.

Try to 'ignore' early labour for as long as you can. If you start rushing around, timing contractions and zooming off to the hospital, you'll make labour seem longer. Keep occupied.

The first two–four weeks after the baby comes home can be exhausting. Develop low expectations. As long as you feed the baby and eat, sleep and shower yourself, that's enough. Delegate everything else – or just leave it. If people offer to help, let them. If they don't, ask! Limit guests to people who will help you. Cocoon yourselves for a 'babymoon', where your family learns to fit together again in a different shape.

14. Childbirth education

Which classes are for you?

Childbirth classes will help you to understand the processes of labour and birth. If you are giving birth in a particular hospital, make sure you and your partner attend their classes. These will help you to become familiar with the hospital and the staff there.

In childbirth education classes you will typically explore coping strategies, and techniques such as massage and relaxation, as well as finding out about the physical processes of labour. You will also find out about pain relief options. Meeting other parents-to-be, and giving and receiving peer support, is also invaluable.

Apart from hospital-based classes, there are many other options. When choosing one think about how the philosophies of the class reflect your own outlook on life. Do not be afraid to change if you are unhappy.

Here's an idea for you

Make enquiries about classes as soon as you are pregnant. If you leave it too late you may find there are no available places on your chosen course.

Classes

International Childbirth Educators Association (www.icea.org)
encourage women and their partners to learn about labour so they can
make informed choices.

National Childbirth Trust (NCT)
(www.nctpregnancyandbabycare.com) Held in small groups, these
usually include learning relaxation skills and practising different
positions for labour, as well as information on pain relief and Caesarean
birth. They also cover postnatal issues and newborn care.

Active Birth (www.activebirthcentre.com) encourage women to follow
their instincts and have an active rather than recumbent birth.
Complementary therapies are discussed. Classes are based on using yoga
to strengthen your body in preparing for labour.

Lamaze (www.lamaze-childbirth.com) encourage pain management
through relaxation, visualisation and breathing exercises.

Birthing from Within (www.birthingfromwithin.com) These offer
practical information and a variety of self-discovery techniques such as
birth art exercises. This emphasis is on 'intuitive' birthing.

Birth Works (www.birthworks.com) teach there is no 'right' way to give
birth. Classes are intended to give parents-to-be the confidence to cope,
with an emphasis on birth companions learning how they can
contribute.

HypnoBirthing (www.hypnobirthing.com) This is a 'natural'
childbirthing technique where students learn how self-hypnosis can
reduce fear and pain during childbirth.

15. Don't believe the hype!

Who should you really listen to?

People treat pregnant women as public property, asking intimate questions and making tactless observations so whose advice should you take? Many grandmas-to-be find it impossible not to give advice. Before you dismiss it all as old fashioned, remember she has experience. But remember it's a loooong time since she had a baby, and advice has changed. Women are much more involved in decision making now, and parents have much more choice. Try to remember that your baby is incredibly important to its grandparents, and that their advice is given with the best of intentions. Knowing this may help you to handle things gently, without hurting anyone's feelings.

Your friends will probably offer advice on everything from what to eat, what lotion to use to avoid stretch marks and what to do to

Here's an idea for you

In the face of stupid comments or advice, stay calm. Treat it with humour and a smile. You can get your point across without hurting feelings.

stop it happening again. Luckily, you will also receive lots of loaned goodies from cribs to maternity wear. So put up with the advice, smile and open your hands.

The absolute worst comments are from annoying strangers, the Food Police. In restaurants: 'Should you be eating that cheese? It might not be good for your baby.' In coffee shops: 'Should you be drinking coffee? Caffeine isn't good for babies you know.' People like this should be ignored. (Or mown down with a baby buggy. Your call!)

How to cope checklist
- Listen first – the advice might just be useful!
- Smile and nod – then disregard accordingly.
- Use diversion – just change the subject.
- Educate yourself – read, surf the internet, join an online community. If you are knowledgeable about a subject, you can argue your case better.
- Quote an expert – your midwife or obstetrician.
- Try to be open-minded – you can listen without committing yourself. Try out the seemingly daft advice as long as it isn't dangerous.

16. Getting to know you

Chatting with your bump.

Prenatal psychologists have proven without doubt that babies in the womb react to external and internal stimuli. From an astonishing eight weeks your baby's first nerve endings reach the surface of her body and she can feel sensations. By the sixteenth week, your baby's ears are functioning. She hears the reassuring rhythmic beat of your heart and the blood moving through the placenta. Studies have shown that a baby's heart rate speeds up when she hears her mother's voice sing or speak, and by the time she is born, your baby will recognise your voice.

Play music and sing to your baby. Music provides stimulation for the developing brain, but lullabies are even better. Your voice combined with music is a love song that comforts your baby in utero as well as after birth.

Here's an idea for you

During pregnancy, keep a journal to record your feelings. This will help you to focus on your baby, and in later years you will be able to share it with the new person you are creating to show them how much they were loved even before they were born.

Connecting through the use of deep relaxation is a great way to bond with your baby. Try the following exercise. Wearing loose clothes, sit on cushions or on the bed. Mum should lie back against dad. Close your eyes, and rest your hands on your bump. Dad should encircle mum in his arms and rest his hands on her belly. Breathe deeply and let go of any tension in your body. Picture the baby inside you. Tell your baby and your partner how much you love them. Nestle into your partner and tell your baby that you can't wait to hold her. Spend time visualising the joyous moment she is finally born. When you are ready, slowly bring your awareness back to the room around you, and then open your eyes.

17. Minor health complaints

How to deal with niggling medical problems.

During pregnancy, you can end up with heartburn or constipation – or even both! Help yourself by eating fibre-rich food, and drinking plenty of liquid. Exercise such as walking or swimming also gently stimulates the bowel, which will aid digestion.

Constipation may lead to haemorrhoids or 'piles'. These itch, throb and generally make it hard to sit comfortably. Ease the pain with a pad made from a sandwich bag filled with small quantity of frozen peas wrapped in a flannel. Press this gently against the sore area. Alternatively, soak a sanitary pad in diluted witch hazel and apply to the affected area.

Heartburn can be severe in pregnancy. Your growing baby is putting extra pressure on your stomach, but mainly your hormones are to blame. Try to

Here's an idea for you

To avoid constipation, add extra sultanas, chopped dates and a spoonful of bran to your breakfast cereal or porridge.

manage the problem by eating smaller, more regular meals. If you find a trigger food, avoid it. Avoid lying down after meals as this position can encourage acid reflux. If you get heartburn at night, prop yourself on extra pillows. Ask your healthcare provider before buying a remedy: Pepto-Bismol is specifically not recommended during pregnancy. Some antacids contain a high percentage of sodium, which is dangerous if you have high blood pressure.

You may have noticed increased vaginal discharge since you became pregnant. This is partly due to increased hormones but also to the increased blood flow to the vaginal area. If the discharge is thin, transparent or white and smells inoffensive, it is normal and will increase until the end of pregnancy. If you use a panty liner, ensure it is of the 'breathable', unscented variety to avoid thrush. If you experience genital itching and your discharge is thick, changes colour or smells odd, let your healthcare provider know. You may have thrush. If the discharge is bloody or very watery, it could indicate your waters have broken and you are at risk of pre-term labour. Contact your healthcare provider immediately.

.

18. Myth or magic?

Could complementary therapies be useful during pregnancy?

Always find an accredited therapist and let them know you are pregnant.

Homeopathy A homeopathic therapist aims to treat you holistically, not just for whatever symptom you are seeking relief from. To find an accredited homeopath contact the Society of Homeopaths: www.homeopathy-soh.org or the Institute for Complementary Medicine: www.icmedicine.co.uk

Aromatherapy A session with a qualified aromatherapist is a great way to find out about massage with oils that you could use during labour. Essential oils may be used diluted in a carrier oil, inhaled or added to bathwater. They may also be used to boost energy and reduce stress levels. To find a qualified aromatherapist contact the Complementary Medical Association: www.the-cma.org.uk

Here's an idea for you

Create a homeopathic first-aid postnatal kit that includes arnica cream or tincture for bruising and calendula cream for sore nipples and babies' bottoms.

47

Herbalism Herbs are natural, but that does not make them safe. Making a simple tea from ginger root or mint leaves can be effective in relieving nausea and heartburn. But other herbs should be used with caution. You can find a qualified herbalist at the National institute of Medical Herbalists: www.nimh.org.uk

Osteopathy During pregnancy, your posture changes and your ligaments soften due to hormonal changes. This can lead to aches and pains. An osteopath can treat these aches by gently manipulating different parts of your body such as your neck, lower back and pelvic joints. You can find a qualified osteopath at the General Osteopathic Council: www.osteopathy.org.uk

Reflexology In reflexology, areas on the feet called 'reflex areas' or 'zones' are seen to represent different organs and systems of the body. If a particular area feels painful when it is manipulated, the organ to which it corresponds may be weak. A trained reflexologist can diagnose potential problems. Find a qualified reflexologist at the Association of Reflexologists: www.aor.org.uk

Acupuncture Acupuncture is based on the idea that there is a vital flow of energy (qi) in the body. This energy must flow freely if we are to remain healthy. An acupuncturist stimulates specific points to remove blockages. Acupuncture may be used to bring on labour if you are overdue. Find a qualified acupuncturist at the British Acupuncture Council: www.acupuncture.org.uk

19. Relax!

Getting sleep and destressing.

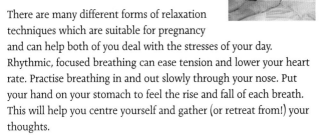

There are many different forms of relaxation
techniques which are suitable for pregnancy
and can help both of you deal with the stresses of your day.
Rhythmic, focused breathing can ease tension and lower your heart
rate. Practise breathing in and out slowly through your nose. Put
your hand on your stomach to feel the rise and fall of each breath.
This will help you centre yourself and gather (or retreat from!) your
thoughts.

Gentle exercise will increase your
general wellbeing, and help you to
sleep better. Exercise at least four
hours before bedtime though, or
you may find you are still on a
high. Yoga is a great, calming and
holistic exercise for pregnancy –
but make sure you take a class
specially designed for pregnant women.

Here's an idea for you

Add a vanilla pod, or a spoonful of
vanilla sugar to warm milk for a bedtime
drink. Have a wholemeal cookie or a
banana with it to keep up your blood
sugar level for an undisturbed night.

49

A professional massage can work relaxation wonders – but make sure you tell your practitioner that you are pregnant. A foot, hand, or neck and shoulder massage or back rub from your partner will go down a treat too.

Sleeping can be hard especially towards the end of pregnancy – but you need all the rest you can get. Restless legs, nocturnal bathroom treks and overheating can all lead to a restless night. Use pillows to support your belly and back at bedtime. Also try a special wedge-shaped pillow to support your bump as you lie on your side.

Warm milk, like so many other homely remedies, has now been proven by scientists to aid sleep. It has been suggested that the amino acid L-tryptophan, found in milk, raises the level of serotonin in your brain, which makes you sleepy. Never take any medication to make you sleep during pregnancy – over the counter or prescription – without first talking to your healthcare provider.

20. Move it, baby!

Tips for safe travel.

The safest time to travel is the second trimester (weeks 14–27). If your vaccinations for travel-related illnesses like typhoid and yellow fever are not up to date, it may be safer to avoid having them during pregnancy. Take no unnecessary risks.

Find out about the medical services available at your destination. Take your medical notes with you and check your travel insurance to make sure that your pregnancy is covered. Trains are a great mode of transport for you. There are loos and a buffet car! Take snacks and drinks of your own, however, to ensure you are getting optimum nutrition.

Boat-wise, be careful. Most cruise lines won't let you travel after 26 weeks. When you call to book your holiday, ask about restrictions for pregnant travellers and check what medical cover they have. Suffering from morning sickness? Boat travel may aggravate it.

Here's an idea for you

If you need medical attention on holiday, tell the doctor that you are pregnant. Make sure you know the word for 'pregnant' in the native language.

Different airlines have different policies about pregnant passengers. Check with the airline and carry documentation stating your due date. A seat in the middle of the plane is probably the smoothest ride, but an aisle seat at the bulkhead gives you more space. Walk about every half hour or so to avoid deep vein thrombosis (DVT). Fasten your belt at pelvic level. Take bottled water to avoid dehydration.

Car travel is probably the most convenient mode of transport for you. Wear your safety belt low and tight across your lap. Push your seat as far back as is comfortable so you are as far away from any airbag action as possible. The impact could harm your baby.

Layer clothing when travelling. Flat shoes with a contoured foot bed are especially great if your feet are swollen. Make sure you have a thick, preferably skid-proof, sole for support.

The rules of pregnancy eating still apply on holiday. Make sure your drinking water – and ice cubes – are safe. If you get diarrhoea, drink plenty of bottled water to replace fluids. See a doctor if it lasts longer than a day – you may need some pregnancy-friendly rehydration therapy.

21. One for the boys

How to be a textbook dad-to-be.

- If your partner is suffering from nausea, make her mint, ginger or weak regular tea. Take it to her in the morning with a couple of crackers or plain biscuits.
- When she says 'Feel the baby – it's kicking', do so gladly. Don't look resigned and give up quickly.
- Make time to attend hospital visits. 'Big' ones, like an ultrasound scan, are especially important.
- Watch a video about childbirth together. Not only does this make you an involved dad-to-be, it also prepares you for some of the 'messier' moments!
- Attend childbirth classes with your partner. That way, you go into the labour suite armed with the right information.
- In the weeks before your baby is due, make sure the car is kept fuelled, and your partner's hospital bags are packed.

Here's an idea for you

Don't forget how that baby was made! It can sometimes feel as though the baby has taken over your life before it is even born. Make time for each other.

- Take responsibility for making things run smoothly at home. Keep the bathroom especially clean. Who wants to throw up in a dirty toilet?
- Learn about the ways you can be involved during labour. You are there not just as a loving partner but also as her 'interpreter' when dealing with medical staff.

Babies aren't breakable. Don't be afraid to hold yours! And remember, the only thing you can't do is breastfeed. Encourage your partner to rest while her body recovers. Get up in the night with the baby when you can. When you go back to work, ring her to let her know you are thinking of her. You also need to know who to call for help and support if you need it – doctor, midwife, health visitor. Your partner will have emotional ups and downs. Be patient and supportive. Let her know she's doing a great job. But don't forget to give yourself a break when you need it too.

22. Meet the parents

Getting used to your new roles.

Nobody is born with parenting skills. We learn to nurture through trial, error and experience. But you do not come to parenting unskilled. As you grew up, you experienced – for better or worse – your own parents' or carers' ways of nurturing. You learned to love friends and build relationships. You fell in love, and nurtured your partner. Hopefully, you learned to love and nurture yourself.

During pregnancy, when your baby arrives or some time later, you will fall in love again – with your baby. The rush of love you experience tears into you with a ferocity previously unimaginable. That doesn't mean parenting isn't hard, or comes naturally; it's something we all have to work at.

Here's an idea for you

Keep a parenting journal to keep in touch with yourself emotionally. You don't have to share this journal with anyone – it is for you.

Think about the parenting styles that were prominent for you during your childhood. How did your parents treat you? How did you feel? Think about a happy day you spent with your parents as a child. Why was it happy? How did your parents act? This exercise will help you to think about the sort of parent you want to be. Compare notes with your partner. One of you may tend to favour stricter or more laissez-faire parenting than the other. The important thing is to open up a dialogue. You and your partner are a team in this parenting journey, and you need to support each other through the sometimes challenging experiences that parenting brings.

New parents – and especially new mothers – have unrealistically high expectations of themselves. We live in a media-fed, 'have-it-all' culture where mothers grind themselves into the ground trying to be some kind of superwoman. There are just not enough hours in the day. Learn to be kind to yourself, or your emotional wellbeing as well as your whole family will suffer.

23. Workplace woes

Coping at work.

You may sail through your pregnancy at work.
Most of us do feel the strain, at least a little.
Help yourself by eating healthily and resting during breaks. If possible,
try to manage your hours so you miss the rush hour. You may be able
to do some of your work from home. Talk to your manager about this.

If you are having trouble with
nausea and vomiting, tell your boss.
Before you tell her, work out what it
is you want – a flexible schedule, say,
until you are past the worst of it? If
you feel really ill, see your doctor.
You may need to take a little time
off. Point out that you are
committed to your work, and the
job will get done – even if it takes
extra work when you feel better.

Here's an idea for you

For more information on working safely
while pregnant, contact the UK Health
and Safety Executive
(www.hse.gov.uk/mothers/) or in the
USA the Organization of Teratology
Information Services
(www.otispregnancy.org).
Your union might also prove useful
(www.otispregnancy.org/)

Make sure you drink plenty of water. Reduce stress levels if possible. If you have a strenuous job, involving a lot of lifting, standing for long periods, etc., ask your employer if you can be temporarily reassigned to a less physical task. Contact your health and safety rep. Heavy work increases your risk of high blood pressure and premature delivery – so be very careful.

If your work brings you into contact with chemicals that are dangerous to developing babies, you must be reassigned. Your baby will otherwise be at risk of developing abnormalities, or even being stillborn. Lead, mercury, many solvents and radiation are among the substances that are dangerous. There are laws requiring employers to protect the health and safety of employees who are (or could be) a new or expectant mother.

24. Who's holding the baby?

The childcare issue.

Whatever decision you make the key is to do what is right for you and your family. It might make more sense for dad to stay at home while the children are small. Working from home allows extra flexibility. Consider this option if one of you has a job where this is possible.

Part-time working can give you the best of both worlds. Too many women find they end up working virtually full-time for part-time wages though, so be careful. You may choose to work full-time. If this is for financial reasons, consider it carefully. Childcare is hugely expensive and the stress of full-time work on top of caring for young children is immense.

Here's an idea for you

Get your child's changing bag and feeds ready the night before. Leave a set of clothes, nappies, toys and other essentials with her carer to save time each morning.

Many mothers go back to work when their baby is around six months old. Unfortunately, this is just about the time when babies start to get anxious with strangers. Phase in separation gradually. Employers offering a crèche are still sadly few and far between.

That leaves a variety of options:

- Grandparents can offer a secure, low-cost option. Make sure you do not take advantage though, and let them know they are appreciated.
- Childminders care for children in their own home. They are inspected and have safety checks. The cost varies – as does the quality of the minders. Get a list of childminders from your local council, and ask around to see if any good local minders have vacancies.
- Nurseries may be private or run by the local authority. These are usually more expensive than childminders and do not offer the same homely setting.
- A nanny is expensive but may be an option if you have two or more children, or you 'nanny share' with another family. Ask to see qualifications and references, and follow them up.
- If you have school-age children, or you work from home, an au pair may be a good option. They may have no formal childcare training (or possibly experience) but can just bridge the gap to give you breathing space to work.

25. Testing...testing...

Assessing the risks of prenatal tests.

Prenatal testing has become a huge part of pregnancy care. But many of the tests carry risks in themselves, so be clear about what you would do if the tests show there is a problem. Before you agree to any test, find out about it in detail. Understand how it is administered, and any associated risks.

Ultrasound Ultrasound scanning uses sound waves to create a 'picture' of your baby. It may be used to date your pregnancy and to find any developmental problems. At 18–20 weeks, a detailed ultrasound scan can check the position of your placenta and the amount of amniotic fluid. Your baby's spine, limbs, head, heart and other internal organs can also all be seen on the scan.

Chorionic villus sampling (CVS)
At 10–12 weeks, an ultrasound scan is used to guide a fine, hollow needle to remove a small piece of the developing placenta. The cells

Here's an idea for you

Before you have any test done, discuss with your partner what you would do if you found an abnormality in your baby. You may decide not to have any tests at all, or to have the less 'invasive' ones.

removed are grown and tested for a variety of abnormalities such as Down's syndrome. CVS does not provide information on neural tube defects such as spina bifida. CVS carries a risk of miscarriage of approximately 2–5%, and some research has implicated the test in causing limb abnormalities in babies.

Amniocentesis An ultrasound scan is used to guide a needle through your abdominal wall and into the amniotic sac. Amniotic fluid, which contains cells from your baby, is removed and tested for abnormalities. The test is carried out at around 15–18 weeks. It may be up to four weeks before you get the result, and by this time you will be feeling your baby move. Any abortion you seek at this stage would be traumatic and possibly painful. Rarely, some types of foetal damage have been reported with amniocentesis. It is currently accepted that amniocentesis carries a risk of miscarriage of between 1 and 2%. New research from one hospital, however, found that amniocentesis diagnosed about 100 babies with Down's syndrome each year, but resulted in the miscarriage of 400 healthy foetuses. Amniocentesis may feel uncomfortable, and you may feel some cramping afterwards.

Maternal serum screening (triple test) The 'triple test' is a blood test that identifies the presence of chemicals that may indicate a risk of certain abnormalities: unconjugated oestriol (uE3), human chorionic gonadotropin (hCG) and alpha-foetoprotein (AFP). The measurement of these chemicals, along with your age and the age of the baby, is used to calculate the risk of having a baby with Down's syndrome.

If your baby has a neural tube defect such as spina bifida, larger amounts of AFP are detected in your blood sample. If your baby has Down's syndrome, the AFP level is lower than normal. However, a higher than average AFP level might also indicate the presence of more than one baby. Low levels can simply mean that your baby is younger than was previously thought.

Do not panic if your triple screen seems to show an abnormality: 96–98% of women who receive a positive triple screen result go on to have babies with no abnormality. However, having a triple result that suggests there may be a problem may push you into having an invasive test, such as an amniocentesis, that you would not have otherwise considered.

26. And baby makes four...or five...

Breaking the news to your other children.

The most important thing is to make your children feel that they are part of the pregnancy right from the outset.

School-aged children may be interested in how the pregnancy works – how the baby gets 'food' in the womb for example. Your child may ask how the baby got there and how it will get out. Think ahead and discuss with your partner what your strategy will be. You may like to have a book ready of pictures of a baby in the womb to help you explain. Ask your child questions first, to elicit what they already know – and what they want to know.

Be careful about the terms you use. If you tell your child that you have a baby in your tummy, she may

Here's an idea for you

Buy plain baby vests or t-shirts and give one to each of your children. Set out some fabric paint and fabric crayons. Ask the children to decorate a t-shirt for their new brother or sister, encouraging them to discuss what things they will show and teach the baby.

think that the baby is in there covered in food! Even a young child can be told that the baby is growing in your uterus, which can be described as a special place in a mother's body where the baby stays until it is ready to be born.

A younger child may be oblivious to the fact that mum is getting rounder and is feeling tired, or possibly sick. Even once told, they often forget. Casually mention the baby in passing, to raise awareness – talk about when the baby will arrive – after the summer holidays, after Christmas, etc. – relating it to an event will make it more understandable to a young child.

27. Practice makes perfect

The second and subsequent pregnancies.

Having a second and third child differs from having your first. Some parents find that the anticipation is not quite the same. Physically, a second and subsequent pregnancy is different to a first. You will 'show' sooner. Your uterus has stretched before and your muscle tone may not be as tight. You'll feel your baby move about a month earlier for the same reason. You may also feel Braxton–Hicks contractions earlier, and they may feel stronger than first time round. Emotionally, you may feel a little distant from this pregnancy. You are focusing hard on the child you already have, and may be worried about loving another child as much as you adore your firstborn.

You may feel a bit of a fraud, but attend childbirth classes again. Some hospitals and birthing centres even run 'refresher' courses for multiparas (that's you – someone who has already had a

Here's an idea for you

Dads, once the baby arrives, try to make special time for each child. Take your older one on the 'nappy and breast pad' run and come back via the park. Snuggle up at bedtime to read him a story.

baby). You may feel anxious about labour if anything did not go according to plan last time. Birthing classes will give you and your partner time to focus on how you might want the birth to be different this time round.

Dads
You may worry that you can't possibly love number two as much as number one. You look forward to coming home from work and playing with your little friend. This one will cry, poo...and that's about it, really. Actually, it will just be different. Make time exclusively for the baby by being in charge of bathtime, for example. Or run short errands and take the baby with you between feeds. That will give your partner time alone with her firstborn and you the chance to bond with your new offspring!

28. The end is nigh...

What to expect at the end.

You might have backache – due to your relaxing
muscles and joints, coupled with the sheer
weight of your baby and bump. A massage and a warm bath can help.
Pelvic tilts – rolling your pelvis backwards and forwards rhythmically –
will ease discomfort. If you get leg cramps drink plenty and have a
gentle stretching session before bed. Don't point your toes.

As your baby grows and puts pressure on your diaphragm you may
find yourself getting breathless. An iced drink can help – or conversely,
a warm one! Changing position can cause your baby to shift a little,
reducing pressure.

Braxton-Hicks contractions can
come hard and fast as your uterus
limbers up for the birth. Try
changing positions, walking about
slowly, taking a warm bath, or
breathing exercises for relief. Call
your healthcare provider if you
think this may be the 'real thing'.

Here's an idea for you

Get yourself a wheat 'cushion' to help
with aches and pains. You can warm
them in an oven or microwave for a
soothing compress to ease back or
pubic pain.

Defining idea

Your pubic area can get really sore due to the relaxation of your joints. A warm compress can help. If symptoms persist, see your midwife. You may be suffering from symphysis pubis dysfunction, a painful condition where the joint at the front of the pelvic bone separates.

As your baby drops down into your pelvis you may experience a constant pressure. This is a real (if uncomfortable) sign that your baby will arrive soon. Being in water can help, as can pelvic tilts.

Heartburn, flatulence and constipation – can get worse in the final stretch. Continue to drink plenty, and eat bland, roughage-filled food. Drinking milk may help.

Keep track of your baby's movements and what seems normal for yours. Healthy babies are active – especially after you have eaten, or had a glass of milk. If you have not felt your baby move all day, drink a glass of milk, lie down and do a 'kick check'. If you do not feel any movements, call your midwife.

29. Coughs and sneezes spread...

What happens if you become ill?

Generally speaking, if you catch a cold, there is little to worry about. The thing to avoid is a high fever as this has been implicated in causing early miscarriages and foetal abnormalities. You are more likely to feel 'stuffed up' during pregnancy, as hormonal changes affect your nasal passages. Your immune system is also affected, so the symptoms may linger longer. If you feel you have flu – achy muscles, headache, fever – call your healthcare provider. Drink plenty of fluid, rest and sponge yourself down with tepid water to reduce your temperature. Your doctor may recommend paracetamol to bring down a fever. It is generally accepted to be the safest painkiller for expectant mothers. Taking aspirin is not recommended. Try to eat regularly. Fresh fruit and yoghurt smoothies will help keep your intake of nutrients high.

Here's an idea for you

Use a steamer or humidifier to try and clear a 'bunged-up' head. A bowl of hot water, with some added fresh mint, and a towel draped over your head will help.

If you get a burning sensation when you pee, or are having to pee even more than usual, you may have a urine infection. Untreated, this could become severe and even lead to premature labour. Consult your doctor. She may prescribe antibiotics. Drink plenty of water. To prevent recurrence, complete your course of antibiotics.

If your vaginal discharge becomes thick and white, like cottage cheese, and you have itching in this area, you may have thrush. You are ten times more likely to suffer in pregnancy. If you think you have it, let your doctor know. She is likely to prescribe pessaries that are safe to use at your stage of pregnancy. Do not use over-the-counter remedies without checking with your doctor. To help yourself, wear cotton knickers and avoid scented bath products. Thrush will not affect your baby unless you have it during labour when there is a chance you could pass it on. This causes white patches and possibly soreness in your baby's mouth, but is easily treatable.

30. Forewarned is forearmed

What happens if there are complications.

Serious complications in pregnancy are thankfully rare. But be aware of potential risks.

If a blood test during pregnancy shows that you have high blood sugar, you may have gestational diabetes. Left untreated, this means you may have trouble delivering vaginally as your baby may be bigger than average. He may also be at higher risk of health problems like respiratory distress syndrome (RDS) or be jaundiced and more likely to grow up obese and develop diabetes. Your doctor will carry out a simple blood test to determine if you have gestational diabetes. If you do, she will suggest a management treatment plan. This will include regular blood tests, a healthy diet and regular exercise. You may need to take insulin. Usually, gestational diabetes goes away after the baby is born.

Here's an idea for you

If your doctor thinks you may have placental abruption, lie on your left side to improve the flow of oxygen and nutrients to your baby. Lying on your back restricts this flow.

Pre-eclampsia affects about one in ten pregnancies. It develops in the second half of pregnancy. Rarely, it can start during labour, or just after your baby is born. Pre-eclampsia causes circulation problems. Symptoms are a bad headache, blurring or seeing flashing lights, high blood pressure, protein in your urine and sudden swelling. See your midwife or doctor without delay if you have two or more of these symptoms. Pre-eclampsia can worsen very quickly – and can be dangerous. In severe cases, you can have fits. Your baby may not be able to get enough oxygen or food from the placenta. If untreated, it can cause the death of both you and your baby.

Placenta praevia is where the placenta covers part, or all, of your cervix. About one in 250 pregnant women have this problem. It is a serious condition, which can cause heavy, usually painless, bleeding and threatens the health of you and your baby. If you have previously had a Caesarean section, are carrying more than one baby or have had a pregnancy with placenta praevia before, you have an increased risk. If you are diagnosed with placenta praevia after the twentieth week, but you're not bleeding, you'll be advised to take life easily. If you start to bleed, you'll be admitted to hospital. You will probably be kept there until your baby is born.

Placental abruption happens when your placenta deteriorates and separates from the wall of your uterus. This is dangerous for you, because of the severity of the bleeding. It can also cause premature labour, or even the death of your baby as she does not get the oxygen or nutrients she needs. If your doctor suspects placental abruption, she will give you an ultrasound scan. If your baby's heart rate is strong and the separation of the placenta is small, your doctor will advise bed rest and may prescribe medication to stop any contractions. You may be given steroid injections to mature your baby's lungs. If the placenta continues to separate, your doctor will suggest an amniocentesis to check your baby's lungs. If your doctor thinks your baby's lungs are capable of functioning outside your womb, your baby will be delivered by Caesarean section.

31. Feathering the nest

Preparing a nursery.

For the first few months, your baby is likely to sleep in your room in a crib for convenience for night feeds. If you have a small flat, you have little choice about where the nursery will be. But if you have options, there are a few things to think about before selecting which room to use.

Choose a room near your own. You don't want a trek for night feeds. Think about which way the room faces, too. Babies nap several times a day and the amount of sunlight might affect the amount your baby sleeps unless you invest in heavy curtains.

Try to choose a room that is quiet – not facing the road, for example. You don't need a great deal of furniture in your nursery. A crib or Moses basket for your room, a cot

Here's an idea for you

Fit safety covers over your electrical sockets. That way you won't have a sudden unpleasant surprise one day as your newly crawling baby decides to lick the smooth white plastic with the interesting metal holes...

for the nursery and somewhere to keep the baby's clothes. Changing-tables are a waste of money. You can't use them for long.

Don't feel you are letting your baby down if you have a small budget and can't buy all the things you see in magazines as 'essentials'. They aren't and your baby won't notice. You can always buy things second hand. Pristine baby equipment and cute nursery furniture fills the 'for sale' section of every newspaper. Be sure to check that any second-hand cot is safe. Any vertical bars should be close enough together so that your baby cannot get trapped between them. Buy a new mattress for hygiene.

Put the cot against an inside wall for warmth and look for hazards. Don't put it near anything your baby could pull down on herself – she will be moving about sooner than you can imagine!

32. Top gear

The best nursery equipment.

A baby sling is a great way to carry your baby from birth and reduce arm strain! It is also useful if you have a toddler, as you can transport both without a heavy twin buggy.

Choose a pram or stroller to fit your lifestyle. You want something that will last for this baby – and any more you might have. The pram or buggy must be suitable for a newborn who needs to lie completely flat. It must be padded, comfortable and weatherproof. If you're going to be using public transport, you'll need one that is light, so you can lift it on and off with one hand and be folded quickly.

Pushchairs and prams can be complicated, so have a go at folding and unfolding it at the shop. Also think about size – will it fit in your car etc? A well-fitting car seat is a legal obligation. Make sure

Here's an idea for you

Buy as much as you can second hand. Check the item is safe by checking up-to-date safety information. Various government websites can help. Check out www.dti.gov.uk/ccp/topics1/safety.htm (UK) and www.cpsc.gov (USA)

you buy one that is suitable for your baby's stage of development.
Ideally buy a new one to make sure it has not been damaged.
Choose one that is padded, comfortable and easy to fit and remove.
You can buy infant-only seats and then a toddler one, or buy one
that will last for several years. Later on, you'll need a booster seat,
for children from age four.

At home...

The first chair you buy is likely to be a bouncer chair, which props
up the baby and allows her to see what is going on. Her back is
supported and any movement she makes creates 'bounce' as the
frame allows her to move.

A high chair is useful from around six months. Whatever model you
choose, check the tray is a good size with high edges. And ensure it
is easy to clean!

33. That's another fine mess...

The lowdown on nappies.

Disposable nappies are convenient and keep babies very dry. Your baby will use 6,000–8,000 nappies before you've got him potty trained and it has been estimated to take up to 500 years to decompose in landfill sites. In addition to the environmental impact, they are expensive. Disposables are incredibly absorbent, however, and help reduce nappy rash. Buy them in bulk: it's cheaper. Some manufacturers even sell the largest packs in plastic storage bins, which are also useful for toy storage.

Cloth nappies are the alternative. Despite their 'green' image, they also have a human and environmental cost. Has the cotton been 'fairly traded'? And how are you going to clean them? This takes water, chemicals and energy. One major plus, however, is that they don't clog up landfill sites. Cloth nappies, can be bulky and leaky for newborns. You need fasteners and

Here's an idea for you

You'll need bags to put disposables in, or to take soiled fabric nappies home from outings. Supermarket cast-offs do the job just as well as fragranced and coloured specialised ones.

nappy liners, which may be
disposable or fabric. These are used
inside cloth nappies to catch poo.
You also need plastic pants. They
keep clothes and bedding dry – but
can keep babies wet so be wary of
nappy rash. (Tip: the muslin sheets
used as nappy liners are great for draping over your shoulder after
feeds to save your clothes from milk dribbles and baby vomit.)

You can also buy fitted cloth nappies, which look and act very much
like a disposable. They are more expensive than the traditional
nappies and take longer to dry due to their thick wadding. You buy
liners to go inside and an outer casing. If you use fabric nappies,
you'll also need a nappy bucket with a lid, plus tongs and a nappy
sanitizer. The initial outlay is expensive, but you'll save money over
time.

From an environmental point of view, a nappy service – using fabric
nappies that are collected from you and washed before returning –
may be the best option as they are washing many nappies at once.
This makes for energy-efficient laundering – although this does not
come cheap.

34. Breastfeeding

Breast is best.

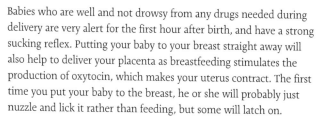

The World Health Organisation recommends that, if possible, mothers should exclusively breastfeed for at least the first four to six months of a baby's life.

Babies who are well and not drowsy from any drugs needed during delivery are very alert for the first hour after birth, and have a strong sucking reflex. Putting your baby to your breast straight away will also help to deliver your placenta as breastfeeding stimulates the production of oxytocin, which makes your uterus contract. The first time you put your baby to the breast, he or she will probably just nuzzle and lick it rather than feeding, but some will latch on.

The whole key to breastfeeding is 'latching on'. When a baby does this correctly, it takes a large mouthful of the breast including the nipple and areola. If your baby just takes the end of your nipple, it will hurt you and he will not get much milk.

Here's an idea for you

Remove the nipple from your baby's mouth by inserting your little finger into the corner of his mouth to release the suction. Don't just pull, or your nipple will ping out of the baby's mouth like a piece of elastic. Ouch!

Cradle your baby in your arm, face turned to your breast. Support your breast with your other hand. Put your index finger above your nipple and your middle finger below your nipple. Tickle the centre of your baby's bottom lip with your nipple. This will make him open his mouth wide and root eagerly. Aim your nipple slightly towards the roof of his mouth and bring your baby towards you, chin first. If your nipples get sore, it may be due to incorrect positioning.

Nurse regularly and on demand. This stimulates your milk supply. Even if your baby is premature, you can still breastfeed. You can pump and take your milk to the hospital to be fed to your baby. The protection your milk offers is invaluable.

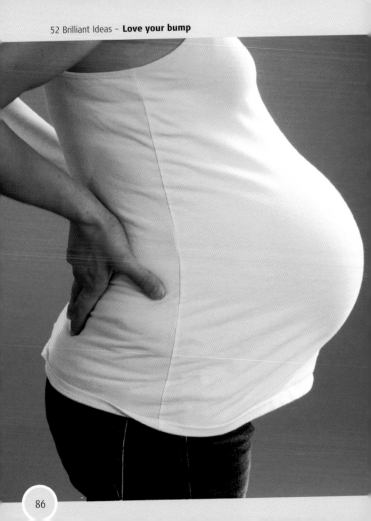

35. Are you in labour?

Sometimes it's hard to tell...

You will begin to feel Braxton-Hicks 'practice' contractions at around the twentieth week of pregnancy. Your uterus tightens and can feel uncomfortable. Braxton–Hicks can last from 30 seconds to over 2 minutes, and tend to last longer and feel stronger as you come closer to giving birth. If they bother you, try walking around slowly to relieve the discomfort.

Real, early labour pains can feel like period cramps and backache. You may feel a band of tightening at the top of your stomach, which spreads downwards. Your belly feels hard to the touch as you experience the contraction.

As your cervix begins to thin and open, ready for the birth, a blood-tinged plug of mucous slides out. This is sometimes known as the 'bloody show'. The plug previously

Here's an idea for you

There are a few other indicators to watch out for that can help you to decide if you are in labour. You may, for example, lose up to a kilo and a half in weight just before. You may feel the famous 'nesting instinct'. You may also have diarrhoea immediately before labour begins.

sealed your cervix and kept your baby safely sealed in, away from infection. This can actually happen a couple of weeks before labour begins, so don't panic. If, however, your discharge is bright red or you just start bleeding, go directly to the hospital, calling an ambulance to take you there. This could be a symptom of premature separation of the placenta (placenta praevia) and is a medical emergency.

Your 'waters' – the sac of amniotic fluid that surrounds your baby – can break at the onset of labour, or actually during labour. They can break in a trickle, as the baby's head plugs the gap, or in a flood. Once your waters have broken, it's a good idea to ring your midwife for advice. There is a risk of infection as your womb is no longer sealed. If your waters break and the fluid is coloured, your baby may be distressed and you should call the midwife immediately.

36. Bag of tricks

Packing your labour kit.

Even if you are having a home birth, a labour
kit is useful. Pack everything in a case and keep
it to hand. Should you have to transfer to hospital, your bag will be
ready. Pack it a couple of weeks before your due date – you never
know!

For mum
Birth plan • Massage oil • Socks – your feet can get cold! • Lollipops
or boiled sweets for energy and to help keep your mouth moist •
Toothbrush, toothpaste • Tie-backs for long hair • Battery-operated
hand fan • Tapes/CDs • Your own pillow – strangely comforting •
Electrolyte sports drinks or water.

If you are staying in hospital
Books, magazines, etc. • Two
nursing bras if breastfeeding •
Breastpads • Baggy knickers –
several pairs for each day • Heavy
flow sanitary towels. You can't use
tampons after the birth because of

Here's an idea for you

You need to take a car seat to the
hospital to bring your precious bundle
safely home. Practise fitting and
removing the car seat several times as a
'dry run' before you actually need it.
Make sure you know how to strap the
baby in and release him or her.

the risk of infection • One or two nightgowns or T-shirts • Thin bathrobe • Slippers • Wash bag • Cosmetics • Phone card • Loose outfit for going home.

For dad
A change of t-shirt – it gets steamy/messy in there • Toothbrush, facecloth, deodorant – for a quick freshen up • Shaving equipment – you may be there for some time • High-energy snacks • Drinks – electrolyte sports drinks to sustain your energy levels • Phone numbers • Mobile phone – for use outside hospital or phonecard • Camera, film and batteries • Camcorder • Swimsuit. In case your partner uses a birthing pool.

For baby
Even if you are using cloth nappies, use tiny disposables in hospital. You will not believe what meconium (the first bowel motions a baby makes) looks like – and what it does to fabric.
• Two all-over vests – the type with popper under the bottom • Hat
• Booties • Soft blanket or shawl.

37. Happy birthday!

The stages of labour.

In early labour your cervix is thinning out and
dilating, opening from 0–3 cm (1.5 inches).
Contractions last about 30–45 seconds and can be irregular. If you
are going to a birthing centre or hospital, stay at home for this phase
to make labour seem shorter. Update your midwife. If you are
birthing at home, potter about, staying upright as much as possible
to allow gravity to help your baby's descent, but rest if you need to.

Partners – get ready! Time and record contractions. Be there to
make sure your partner has everything she needs. If you are going to
hospital, make sure her bag and the car keys are to hand. If you
need sitters for your children, call now.

In the 'active' phase: your cervix
will continue to dilate from 4–7 cm
(1.5–3 inches). Contractions are
stronger, closer together and last
longer – perhaps 45–60 seconds. If
you are going to hospital, make a
move. Continue with your
breathing techniques, and change your position regularly.

Here's an idea for you

Guys – if your partner feels
overwhelmed or panicky, touch her so
she feels connected. Make eye contact,
bringing your face close to hers.

As a partner, go into full support mode! Take your cues from her. Tell her how well she's doing.

The 'transition phase': this is the worst stage. Your cervix is dilating to the last few centimetres, from 7– 10 cm (3–4 inches). Contractions are strong, lasting 60–80 seconds, and are close together. You may feel irritable and disorientated. This intense stage is short. Deal with one contraction at a time. It's nearly over! Try not to be offended by anything she says or does now! Offer lavish praise.

The moment of truth: You will suddenly get an overwhelming urge to push. As your baby's head reaches the opening of your vagina – you'll feel a painful burning sensation. Pant through this and allow the baby's head to ease out. Your baby's head will be delivered, then shoulders, then the rest slithers out. All that is left is the delivery of the placenta and a clean up. If you had an episiotomy or a tear, you will be stitched up.

38. The pain

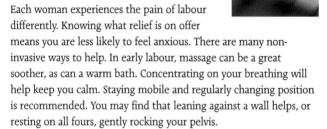

Dealing with labour pains.

Each woman experiences the pain of labour differently. Knowing what relief is on offer means you are less likely to feel anxious. There are many non-invasive ways to help. In early labour, massage can be a great soother, as can a warm bath. Concentrating on your breathing will help keep you calm. Staying mobile and regularly changing position is recommended. You may find that leaning against a wall helps, or resting on all fours, gently rocking your pelvis.

Transcutaneous electrical nerve stimulation (TENS) can help. To use a TENS machine, adhesive pads are attached to your back. A low-voltage electric current is passed through the pads making your body produce endorphins, natural pain-relieving substances. It takes about 30 minutes before you feel any effect, so it is worth using in early labour. TENS machines have no reported side effects for mothers or babies.

Here's an idea for you

Practise relaxation breathing exercises before you go into labour – make it part of your relaxation routine – this works in times of stress for non-pregnant people too.

Entonox (gas and air) is a mixture of oxygen and nitrous oxide (laughing gas). For the pain relief to work you need to start breathing in the gas as soon as you feel a contraction start. It may give you a dry mouth, so sip water between breaths of gas.

If the pain is unbearable, painkilling injections such as diamorphine, pethidine and meptazinol can help. These drugs take around 20 minutes to work, and the effects last between two and four hours. These drugs do have side effects - they can make you drowsy, nauseous and can slow your breathing down. They are not usually given too close to the actual birth as they can make the baby drowsy too.

An epidural gives excellent pain relief but may have side effects. Blood pressure can get low so a drip is routinely set up. This, along with the need for a foetal heart monitor and a catheter, means you are confined to bed. Rarely, spinal fluid can leak, causing headache and backache. An epidural is useful if a woman has a Caesarean section, as she may stay awake throughout.

39. Lady in waiting

Can you kick-start labour?

According to childbirth expert Sheila Kitzinger, 95% of babies do not arrive on their due date. A post-mature pregnancy is one that is longer than 42 weeks. Most pregnancies last 38–42 weeks. About 5% of pregnancies are post-term. If your cycle is irregular, you may have conceived later than you imagine.

It is vital to ensure your baby is truly post-mature before he or she is induced. If your dates are calculated incorrectly, your baby may be born prematurely. Genuine post-maturity can endanger your baby, however, so induction may become necessary.

When your due date comes and goes, keep yourself busy. Try a few ways to get the ball rolling. Like sex! An orgasm will produce oxytocin, the hormone that causes

Here's an idea for you

Check how much your baby is moving with a 'kick check'. Decreased movement may mean your baby is not thriving. A baby who has seriously slowed movements may be at risk of stillbirth. Get medical help.

contractions. Semen contains prostaglandins, which can help to soften your cervix so that labour begins. Sounds clinical, but could be fun...

If your pregnancy lasts one week or more past your due date, your healthcare provider will check in regularly. An ultrasound may be done to check the amount of amniotic fluid around your baby. Once overdue, there is a risk that your placenta will become less efficient and your baby will be at risk. Your midwife will check the baby's heartbeat, and your cervix for thinning and dilation. Your doctor will probably suggest induction once you are two weeks past your due date. This is done to avoid foetal distress, where your baby doesn't get enough oxygen.

There are several medical methods used to induce birth.

- Breaking your waters. The sac of amniotic fluid is ruptured with an instrument that looks like a large crochet hook. This is uncomfortable but it doesn't hurt.
- Prostaglandin gel. A blob of gel is put high in your vagina to help soften your cervix.
- Syntocinon drip. Once your waters have been broken, an intravenous drip containing syntocinon can be used to make your uterus contract. If your labour does not progress after this, you may need a Caesarean.

40. Tiny treasures

Going into labour early...

Pre-term labour occurs when a baby is born three weeks or more before the expected due date. The following can only begin to describe the actual experiences of premature birth.

You are at risk of delivering prematurely if you:

- Have a history of early contractions and have delivered a previous premature baby (an increased risk of 20–40%).
- Are having a multiple pregnancy.
- Live or work in a stressful environment.
- Have a vaginal or cervical infection that was not treated effectively.
- Have had two or more urinary infections during the pregnancy.
- Drink alcohol, smoke or take recreational drugs.
- Have a history of three or more abortions or miscarriages that were treated with D&C. This can weaken the cervix.

Here's an idea for you

If your baby is less than 34 weeks, he probably will be fed intravenously. You can still take breast milk to the hospital to be fed to your baby. Some hospitals even have milk banks where mothers donate milk for premature babies.

- Have diabetes.
- Have high blood pressure.
- Have pre-eclampsia.

Go to hospital immediately if you have a gush of fluid, are bleeding, have a series of contractions or feel as though a period is about to start.

It may be possible to slow down or even stop your labour. There are drugs to stop contractions. If your baby is younger than 34 weeks, you will probably be given steroid injections to help mature your baby's lungs. Remember, due to medical advances, babies born early have an increasingly greater chance of surviving and developing without any long-term problems.

If your baby is born prematurely, his outlook is affected by the gestational age, size, availability of specialist care and whether the baby is found to have any health problems that developed in the womb.

If your baby is less than 23 weeks, he almost certainly won't survive. But by 24 weeks, just under half of all babies survive. Any extra time spent in the womb is invaluable. A baby born at 25 weeks has a higher than 50% chance of survival. By 26 weeks, it's 75%, and by 28 weeks, 85% of babies survive. If your baby is born at 35 weeks, he may still have to spend a little time in special care, but he should be fine.

A paediatrician or neonatologist will attend your delivery to resuscitate your baby. Once he is stable, he will be transferred to a neonatal intensive care unit (NICU). If you give birth at a small hospital, you may need to transfer to a larger one with more facilities. Many premature babies need to be on a ventilator to help them breathe. He may develop respiratory distress syndrome (RDS) because of his immature lungs.

It is also likely that your baby will receive antibiotics, as infections are a common reason for premature births. He will also be given intravenous fluids. He is also likely to be hooked up to a cardiorespiratory monitor. All this can look frightening. Take each hour as it comes and then each day. Stay close by and keep asking questions.

41. Too posh to push?

The C section question.

It's been said that the increasing number of celebrity mums having elective sections for cosmetic reasons is driving other women to do the same. An elective Caesarean should only be carried out for medical reasons, after full discussion with your healthcare provider.

In some situations a Caesarean may be the safest option for mother and baby. This may be discussed in advance and an elective (planned) section may be carried out, one to two weeks before your expected due date (EDD). An emergency section may be carried out when complications develop during delivery.

A section may be safest if:

■ You have placenta praevia, where your placenta develops low down and covers your cervix.

■ You have vaginal bleeding and cannot deliver naturally.

■ Your cord prolapses.

Here's an idea for you

A Caesarean section should not prevent you from breastfeeding. Put a pillow across your lap to guard your wound, and put another alongside your buttock and thigh on the side you intend to feed first.. Hold your baby's head in the palm of your hand, and encourage him/her to latch on.

- You have pre-eclampsia.
- Your baby is premature, but needs to be delivered.
- You have an active case of genital herpes.

During a Caesarean a cut is made across your lower abdomen. Your womb is opened and your baby is lifted out. Your placenta is delivered, and the obstetrician closes the incision. The operation generally takes between 20 and 30 minutes.

If possible, an epidural is given. This means you stay awake during the operation, so can welcome your baby. Your partner may also be present. You may feel some pressure and 'rummaging' during the Caesarean, but will not feel pain. If the section is an emergency you may be advised to have a general anaesthetic. After the anaesthetic wears off, any pain can be controlled with painkillers. The drugs chosen are safe for breastfeeding.

Most women are up and about within 24 hours. Most leave hospital four or five days later but will need support for up to six weeks after the birth, as they will not be able to lift things, etc., until their wound has healed.

42. Salad tongs and suction cups

Birthing instruments.

Many women who have had assisted deliveries have felt that they did not know enough about the procedures to make informed choices. As forceps and ventouse extraction is only used when there is a problem, you may feel that you are being swept along by events.

Why are women given assisted deliveries?

- Breech babies are often delivered with forceps. The baby's body is born and then the forceps are put round her head to draw it out carefully.
- 'Failure to progress': your baby's head is not moving down through your pelvis.
- An epidural has relaxed your pelvic floor muscles too much.
- Your baby is in a difficult position, e.g. face up.
- You are exhausted and unable to push any more.
- Your baby has become distressed and needs delivering fast.

Forceps

You'll be given a local anaesthetic unless you already have an epidural. You will put your legs in stirrups and have a catheter inserted into your bladder. You'll be given an episiotomy, and the forceps (instruments that look like a bit like salad servers) are eased into your vagina. The obstetrician will use them to pull gently as you have a contraction. If your baby is not born soon, you may need a Caesarean section. A paediatrician will probably be present to care for your baby after birth. Apart from the episiotomy and any tears, you are likely to be bruised and sore. Your baby may be a little bruised and initially her head a bit misshapen.

Ventouse

A ventouse is a suction cup that is attached to your baby's head to help deliver her. You will put your legs in stirrups and have a catheter inserted into your bladder. The obstetrician will attach the cup to your baby's head, then suck the air out of the cap using a pump. Once the cap is fixed, the obstetrician will ask you to push with your next contraction while he pulls. If your baby is not born soon, you may need a Caesarean.

You may feel confused about what happened and be frightened that it could happen again. Talk to your healthcare provider after the birth. Request a meeting with the obstetrician so she can explain what happened – and why.

43. The unkindest cut?

The truth about episiotomy.

An episiotomy is a cut made in your perineum – the skin between your vagina and your anus – in order to deliver your baby. Often, if a woman tears during delivery, it is as a result of her position. Being flat on your back is the worst. Lying on your side is thought to be the best for avoiding episiotomy. Only push as your body tells you to. As your baby's head stretches your perineum, you will feel a burning sensation. Raise your chin and blow quickly and lightly, allowing your baby's head to slide out slowly.

The best way to avoid an episiotomy is to do ten minutes of perineal massage daily in your last trimester: Wash your hands and keep your fingernails short. Sit on your bed. Bend your knees up, and let your legs flop apart. Lubricate your fingers with olive oil. Spread

Here's an idea for you

A water birth reduces the risk of episiotomy. But the most important thing is the attitude of your obstetrician. Ask her what proportion of births she gets the scissors out for? If it's more than 20%, ask why.

oil on your perineum, being careful not to touch your rectum and then your vagina as you may transfer bacteria and cause infection. Insert your thumbs into your vagina, pressing them against the back wall. Gently sweep them away from each other up the walls of your vagina. Repeat for several minutes. Next, gently rub your perineum between your thumb and forefinger. Your thumb should be inside your vagina and your index finger on the outside, with your perineum between them. Relax your muscles as you do this.

Kegel exercises will help to strengthen your pelvic floor muscles. Honed pelvic floor muscles will make pregnancy and birth easier, and you are more likely to avoid a tear or an episiotomy. To find the correct muscles, pretend you're trying to stop peeing. Don't tighten your stomach or thigh muscles at the same time. Do not hold your breath. Then try this exercise: Imagine there is a tiny elevator inside your vagina! Imagine it rising through each storey. As it ascends, draw up your muscles a little more without losing any of the accumulating tension. Once you get to the 'top floor', slowly start the journey back down. Repeat for around five minutes.

44. How do you feel?

Emotions run high.

The rollercoaster of feelings is only partly due
to your hormones. Mainly, it is because you are exhausted and can't
think straight. Apart from recovering from the birth itself, there are
all the night feeds and the hours spent 'settling' your baby.

This is the best piece of advice in the whole book, so read it carefully.
Make sure you nap whenever the baby does. Don't use the time to
tidy up or sort things out – sleep. If people ask if they can help, ask
them to take the baby for a walk in the buggy, and sleep some more.

Baby blues

The 'baby blues' typically occur in
the first few hormonally charged
days after birth. Symptoms
include:

- Feeling sad.
- Crying. Your hormones make
  you feel weepy, as does the
  realisation that babies are for life.

Here's an idea for you

If your partner is feeling weepy,
reassure her. She may feel embarrassed
if it is out of character. Encourage her
to sleep as much as possible. Tell her
what a wonderful mother she is. Let her
know you are in this together.

- Being oversensitive. Yes, you may be being a bit 'touchy'!
- Feeling anxious. We all keep poking our newborns to make sure they are still breathing…
- Feeling irritable.
- Feeling overwhelmed. All new parents feel this. It's a huge responsibility.

Don't forget your partner and other children in all of this. Try spoiling your husband a little to show him that he still holds the same place in your life – a backrub or a silly gift could be all it takes. Remember to spend quality time with other children – if possible without the new arrival. If they have noticed you being tired and grumpy explain why and tell them you're getting used to having a new baby but everything is going to be fine soon.

45. The strangest bedfellows...

The hospital experience.

Your stay can be anything from as little as 6 hours to 48 hours for a normal birth and between three and five days for a Caesarean. Following your baby's birth on the labour ward, you and your baby will be checked over. About two hours later you will be taken to the postnatal ward.

Reassuringly, midwives are available round the clock. During your stay, a midwife will check your temperature, pulse and blood pressure at least once a day. She will palpate your tummy to make sure your uterus is contracting. She will also ask about blood loss (lochia). For the first few days, this will be like a heavy period. If you pass any large clots, tell her. This is normal, but if it keeps happening

Here's an idea for you

Dads – in the first few days after the birth you should go into 'loving-partner overdrive'. Take your partner presents – not at all baby related!

there is a chance that you have retained some of your placenta. If you had stitches, the midwife will check to ensure they are healing. If you had a Caesarean, she will check your wound. She can also advise on breastfeeding.

Your baby will also be checked regularly – to check for things like jaundice. She will check that his eyes are not sticky – very common – and look at his mouth to rule out thrush. She will show you how to keep the umbilical stump clean and dry.

When you leave you will be given notes to take to your doctor as soon as possible. You are given 24-hour contact numbers so you can talk to a midwife at any time. The community midwife will visit the day after you leave the hospital. She will call every other day until the baby is ten days old. On about day seven, your baby will be given a PKU test. Phenylketonuria (PKU) is a rare genetic disorder. On day ten, your baby will be weighed to see if he has regained his birth weight. If she is happy, the midwife will discharge you to the care of the health visitor. She will visit once or twice, and then you will attend the baby clinic at your local surgery for weighing, developmental checks and immunisation.

46. Bringing baby home

What to expect in the first week after giving birth.

How soon you go home after the birth depends on you and on your hospital's policy. If it is your first baby, you are liable to stay in hospital longer than for subsequent births. Do not feel as though you have to stay. Equally, if you feel unwell, ask to stay longer.

After the excitement of the birth, you may feel rather daunted. Relax – most new mums feel like this and just about all of them manage. Make sure you have company for the first week or so. Things seem less scary when you can run them by someone else. Eat well, rest and take time out while your partner or a relative cuddles the baby. Remember that breastfeeding is a learned skill for you and your baby. Contact a lactation counsellor if you want to. The La Leche League (www.lalecheleague.org/) can be a big help.

Here's an idea for you

Dads, do something really special for when your partner comes home from hospital. It doesn't have to be expensive to be memorable. Festoon the living room with balloons and streamers, for example.

It's great to have visitors, but it can be tiring. Dads should act as a 'shield', encouraging helpful visitors, but putting off those who expect to be entertained.

You will experience heavy blood loss for the first week. In fact, when you get home and are more active, or are breastfeeding, you may find that it is heavier and accompanied by clots. If you suddenly start bleeding heavily or have large clots after the first few days, call your midwife or doctor.

You may also have 'afterpains'. These are more common after the birth of second or subsequent children, and is your womb contracting down to its pre-pregnancy size. You could be hit by the 'baby blues'. This stage of feeling down and a bit inadequate usually only lasts a week or two. If you feel really low, talk to your healthcare provider. You may be suffering from postnatal depression.

47. Getting personal

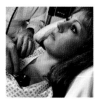

Your postnatal check up.

Some places carry out the check six weeks after you give birth, others at eight weeks. Your doctor will ask routine questions. Are you having any unusual discharge or breast discomfort? Are you feeding the baby yourself? Your doctor will palpate your stomach to make sure your uterus has sunk back into your pelvic cavity. She may check any stitches. She will probably do general physical checks. If you have been feeling unusually tired she may suggest a blood test to check for anaemia.

You may be sent a questionnaire to fill in and take to your check up. This can be a helpful tool in detecting women who are suffering from postnatal depression. Your baby will have his heart, lungs, abdomen and hips checked. He will be weighed and his length and head size will be measured. These measurements will be recorded to show that he is

Here's an idea for you

The postnatal check up is a good opportunity for you to ask anything either about yourself or your baby. Keep a note of any questions. If you have urgent questions, call your doctor or your health visitor.

growing at the expected rate. The doctor will feel the fontanelles (soft spots) on his head to check that they are not bulging or sunken. Boys are examined to see if their testicles are down in the scrotum.

The doctor will ask about your baby's responses. Does he smile and respond to your voice? Does he follow you around the room with his eyes? Your doctor will also check if your baby 'startles' at loud noises. These are indicators that his hearing and eyesight are OK. She will check his muscle tone. She will ask you about his developing head control. She will check for his 'startle' or Moro reflex. The doctor will lift your baby forward with his head supported, then will allow him to drop back suddenly, catching his head in her other hand. Your baby should have a 'startled' look. He will probably cry. It looks like baby torture, but it is a good test that your baby is developing normally. Give him a cuddle and he will soon be calm again. Your doctor will also check your baby's 'grip' or Palmer reflex. After all this, your poor baby will have his first immunisation.

48. The baby blues

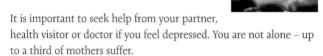

Could you be at risk?

It is important to seek help from your partner, health visitor or doctor if you feel depressed. You are not alone – up to a third of mothers suffer.

Unsurprisingly, you are more at risk of postnatal depression (PND) if you have an unsupportive spouse and a poor support network. Other triggers are financial difficulties, problems with older children or if you have had several babies very close together. If you are in a difficult relationship, or are separating or divorcing, you have an increased risk. If you have had a difficult delivery, you are also more at risk. If you have a history of depression, unrelated to pregnancy, your risk increases. If you are ill, or your baby is unwell, you may also be more likely to become depressed.

Here's an idea for you

Dads, you can help your partner by being loving and understanding – she may be acting very differently to the woman you know and love. She cannot 'snap out of it' and you cannot make her feel better on your own. See your doctor and if necessary seek help from your family and friends.

If you have PND, you may feel overwhelmed by life. You may cry more than usual and be oversensitive. You are likely to feel disproportionately anxious, panicked or hopeless; to feel very tired and have difficulty concentrating. You may feel that you are a 'bad mother'. You may be disinterested in your baby, or overly anxious. You may harbour thoughts about hurting your baby or yourself and feel no one understands. You are likely to feel very tired and want to sleep a great deal.

It is crucial to ask for help if you are experiencing any of these symptoms. Your doctor should be your first port of call. There are also a number of PND support groups that you may find useful. In the UK, for example, the Meet A Mum Association (www.mama.co.uk) and the Association for Postnatal Illness (www.apni.org) are sources of help.

49. Use it or lose it!

Getting back in shape.

The key to embarking on a fitness regime is to
set yourself realistic goals. Don't compare yourself to anyone else –
especially not those celebrities who ping back into shape before they
leave the exclusive maternity hospital. Remember: it took nine months
to have your baby, so give yourself time to get back into shape.

Exercise is the only way to tone muscles. Dieting can make you lose
weight, but it can't strengthen your muscles. You can exercise with
your baby, thereby dispensing wth the need for sitters. It is too easy to
use the 'sitter excuse' to avoid it. Pop your baby in the sling or buggy
and go for brief, but brisk, walks –
you should feel breathy but not
breathless.

Dance with your baby. Put on some
up-tempo music and dance around
with her in your arms or the sling.

Here's an idea for you

You get the same cardiovascular – and
even calorie burning – benefits from
three 10-minute workouts at different
points during the day as you would if
you exercised in one session. Even the
most demanding baby will allow you to
fit this into your schedule.

117

Just choose a fitness activity that you enjoy. Another option is to buy an exercise video to use at home with your baby nearby. You can even work out with your baby. Once your body has healed from the birth and you have been for your postnatal check up, try doing sit-ups with your baby lying on your thighs. Just make sure you hold her carefully. You can also do press-ups with your baby lying on a rug between your hands and your knees.

It's also worth joining an exercise class designed specifically for mums and babies. Childcare isn't an issue if your class includes your baby.

50. Up for it again...?

Sex after childbirth.

Sex may be the last thing on your minds after the birth of your baby. Mum may be tired, sore – and terrified of getting pregnant again. Dad may feel guilty at the pain his partner has gone through. Be patient. There is no 'magic time' for resuming lovemaking. It should happen when both of you are ready.

Ideally, do not have full penetrative sex until after your postnatal check-up. But that date should not be viewed as a 'green light'. Sex will be the last thing on your mind if the baby is not sleeping and your stitches are sore. If you're in any doubt about whether you are physically ready, ask the doctor.

You may feel like messing around a little, but not having full sex. Explain this to your partner. It can be fun, enjoying extended foreplay. This is important for dad, who may feel marginalised

Here's an idea for you

When you are both ready to have sex again, begin gently. It's a good idea to choose a position where the woman can control the pace and depth of penetration – perhaps going on top – to make sure she is physically comfortable and in control.

by all the intimacy between mum and the baby. It is also good for mum, who may have lost confidence in her physical attractiveness.

Generally, your libido will start to rise again within two–three months of having your baby. If it doesn't, talk to your partner and/or doctor.

Hormonal changes can lead to vaginal dryness for the first few months after giving birth. Condoms with a built-in lubricant may help. Or buy a lubricant, such as K-Y Jelly or Senselle. But be careful guys: for the first couple of months after your baby's birth, avoid oral sex with your partner due to the risk of embolism. But that doesn't mean she can't do it to you!

Yes, you have just passed a whole person through your vagina, but don't worry you won't feel 'baggy' to your partner. The vagina is very elastic and snaps back into shape.

51. Brave new world

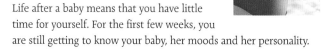

Life as a parent.

Life after a baby means that you have little
time for yourself. For the first few weeks, you
are still getting to know your baby, her moods and her personality.

Don't expect everything to be the blissful, air-brushed image of
parenting that proliferates in some pregnancy magazines. Get rid of
unrealistically high expectations. You are a good parent, but that
does not mean you have to be all-knowing, all-giving and that you
should never feel resentful, frustrated or angry. Parenthood is hard,
and if you treat it as a learning experience that never ends, you'll be
fine.

If this is your first baby, you are
also getting to know yourselves as
parents. That can be odd, as you
see each other in a new light. You
and your partner also have new
roles to play within your extended

Here's an idea for you

Do you wonder what your partner does
all day at home with the baby (and why
the house is a tip)? Try looking after
your daughter for a whole day? Perhaps
now you see that sympathy, not
criticism, is in order.

Defining idea

families – and so do your parents, if this is a first grandchild. Everybody has a bit of mental and emotional shifting around to do at first.

One way to get a life back is to organise a babysitting circle with other 'new parent' friends. Watch how they interact with their own child, so you feel comfortable having them as sitters. Once you have found people you are comfortable with, call on them to see if they can babysit. If they can't, you go on to the next person on the list. Always tell your sitter where you are going and how long you are going to be. And then return the favour.

52. Every parent's nightmare

Miscarriage and stillbirth.

Before 24 weeks, if a baby dies in the womb it is called a miscarriage. After 24 weeks, the death is called a stillbirth. Whatever loss your family experiences, it is devastating. Miscarriages occur for many reasons including infections, hormonal problems and chromosomal abnormalities in the baby. The cause of about 70% of all stillbirths remains uncertain.

Mothers with a baby who has died in the womb face further bad news. They still have to experience labour. Once your baby is born, you may still feel joy at meeting her. You can dress her in a special outfit and take pictures. The midwives may make hand and footprints for you to take home. Do whatever feels right for you.

Here's an idea for you

Find a bereavement counsellor through the hospital or your doctor. Consider writing an open letter to your baby. It may make you cry, but it will give you a chance to say all the things that were left unsaid. You may wish to plant a tree in memory of your child.

You may want to have your baby baptised. Your vicar or priest can do this or you can ask the hospital chaplain. This may not be for you. Again, do whatever feels appropriate. Saying goodbye as you leave the hospital is awful because it is so final. Leave when you are physically ready. Ask a friend to move all the baby things you have collected until you decide what to do with them.

Your vicar or the hospital chaplain can help you make funeral arrangements. Funeral directors often provide a coffin and cremation or burial free of charge for a stillborn baby.

You may want to try again as soon as possible – not to replace the baby that died, but to have a baby to cherish. You may decide to wait or never to try again. You will never forget your baby and will feel sad as anniversaries arrive. But you will learn to live with your loss. To help you grieve, talk to other parents who have had similar experiences. Log on to: www.stillnomore.org/ www.uk-sands.org/ www.tommys.org/

brilliant ideas

This book is published by Infinite Ideas, creators of the acclaimed **52 Brilliant Ideas** series. If you found this book helpful, here are some other titles in the **Brilliant Little Ideas** series which you may also find interesting.

- **Be incredibly healthy:** 52 brilliant little ideas to look and feel fantastic
- **Catwalk looks:** 52 brilliant little ideas to look gorgeous always
- **Drop a dress size:** 52 brilliant little ideas to lose weight and stay slim
- **Enjoy great sleep:** 52 brilliant little ideas for bedtime bliss
- **Get fit!:** 52 brilliant little ideas to win at the gym
- **Healthy children's lunches:** 52 brilliant little ideas for junk-free meals kids will love
- **Incredible sex:** 52 brilliant little ideas to take you all the way
- **Make your money work:** 52 brilliant little ideas for rescuing your finances
- **Quit smoking for good:** 52 brilliant little ideas to kick the habit
- **Raising young children:** 52 brilliant little ideas for parenting under 5s
- **Relax:** 52 brilliant little ideas to chill out
- **Shape up your bum:** 52 brilliant little ideas for maximising your gluteus

For more detailed information on these books and others published by Infinite Ideas please visit www.infideas.com.

See reverse for order form.

Qty	Title	RRP
	Be incredibly creative	£4.99
	Catwalk looks	£5.99
	Drop a dress size	£5.99
	Enjoy great sleep	£5.99
	Get fit	£5.99
	Healthy children's lunches	£5.99
	Incredible sex	£5.99
	Make your money work	£5.99
	Quit smoking for good	£4.99
	Raising young children	£5.99
	Relax	£5.99
	Shape up your bum	£5.99
	Add £2.49 postage per delivery address	
	TOTAL	

Name: ....

Delivery address: ....

....

....

E-mail:............................Tel (in case of problems): ....

By post Fill in all relevant details, cut out or copy this page and send along with a cheque made payable to Infinite Ideas. Send to: *Brilliant Little Ideas*, Infinite Ideas, 36 St Giles, Oxford OX1 3LD. **Credit card orders over the telephone** Call +44 (0) 1865 514 888. Lines are open 9am to 5pm Monday to Friday.

Please note that no payment will be processed until your order has been dispatched. Goods are dispatched through Royal Mail within 14 working days, when in stock. We never forward personal details on to third parties or bombard you with junk mail. The prices quoted are for UK and RoI residents only. If you are outside these areas please contact us for postage and packing rates. Any questions or comments please contact us on 01865 514 888 or email info@infideas.com.